SCHOLASTIC
News
Nonfiction Readers®

Our Earth
Keeping It Clean

by Peggy Hock

Children's Press®
An Imprint of Scholastic Inc.
New York Toronto London Auckland Sydney
Mexico City New Delhi Hong Kong
Danbury, Connecticut

These content vocabulary word builders are for grades 1–2.

Content Adviser: Zoe Chafe, Research Associate, Worldwatch Institute, Washington, DC

Reading Consultant: Cecilia Minden-Cupp, PhD, Early Literacy Consultant and Author, Chapel Hill, North Carolina

Photographs © 2009: age fotostock/Jeff Greenberg: 1, 19; Alamy Images: 2, 4 bottom right, 14 (Rodolfo Arpia), 4 top, 8 right (Nigel Cattlin/Holt Studios International Ltd.), back cover, 17 (Dennis MacDonald), 5 top right, 13 (Alan Oliver), 23 top left (Photo Japan), 15 (The Garden Picture Library), 20 right, 21 left (Worldspec/NASA); Busycle/Heather Clark and Matthew Mazzotta/www.busycle.com: 23 bottom right; Getty Images/Jeff Mermelstein: 5 top left, 9; iStockphoto: 11 (Uli Hamacher), 21 top (Carmen Martinez Banus), 5 bottom left, 6 (Reuben Schulz); NASA/Nick Galante/Dryden Flight Research Center Photo Collection: 23 top right; PhotoEdit: 21 center right (Bill Aron), 20 top left (Robert Brenner), 20 bottom left, 21 bottom (Michael Newman), cover (David Young-Wolff); ShutterStock, Inc.: 7 (Cloki), 5 bottom right, 12 (Coko), 4 bottom left, 8 left (Wrangler); USDA/Keith Weller: 23 bottom left.

Book Design: Simonsays Design!
Book Production: The Design Lab

Library of Congress Cataloging-in-Publication Data
Hock, Peggy, 1948–
Keeping it clean / By Peggy Hock.
    p. cm.—(Scholastic news nonfiction readers)
Includes bibliographical references and index.
ISBN-13: 978-0-531-13832-8 (lib. bdg.) 978-0-531-20432-0 (pbk.)
ISBN-10: 0-531-13832-1 (lib. bdg.) 0-531-20432-4 (pbk.)
1. Pollution—Juvenile literature. 2. Conservation of natural
resources—Juvenile literature. I. Title. II. Series.
TD176.H63 2008
363.73—dc22   2007051894

©2009 Scholastic Inc.
All rights reserved. Published in 2009 by Children's Press, an imprint of Scholastic Inc.
Published simultaneously in Canada. Printed in the United States of America.   44
SCHOLASTIC, CHILDREN'S PRESS, and associated logos are trademarks
and/or registered trademarks of Scholastic Inc.
1 2 3 4 5 6 7 8 9 10 R 18 17 16 15 14 13 12 11 10 09

CONTENTS

WORD HUNT

Look for these words as you read. They will be in **bold**.

chemicals
(**kem**-uh-kuhls)

pollution
(puh-**loo**-shuhn)

rainwater
(**rayn**-waw-tur)

garbage
(**gar**-bij)

litter
(**lih**-tur)

soil
(soyl)

stream
(streem)

Earth Gives Life

Planet Earth gives us everything we need to live.

It gives us water to drink.

It gives us air to breathe.

We grow our food in Earth's **soil**.

soil

This is how Earth's water, land, and air look from space. It is important to keep them clean and healthy.

But people do things that hurt Earth. They make **garbage** and use **chemicals**. Both can make land and water dirty.

People make air dirty too. Burning gas and other things for energy makes air **pollution**.

chemicals

pollution

This garbage was dumped in a place called a landfill. In the wrong places, garbage pollutes land or water.

Air pollution causes many problems.

Dirty air can make people sick. It can also harm animals and plants.

One kind of air pollution is causing Earth to get warmer. This causes problems for living things.

Many power plants burn coal to get energy. This gives people energy that they need. But it also pollutes the air.

Land and water pollution are problems, too.

Some people make land dirty by throwing garbage on it. This garbage is called **litter**.

When it rains, water can carry this litter into a river, **stream**, lake, or ocean.

stream

Water carried litter toward this drain. When the water went down the drain, it left the litter behind.

Some chemicals used on lawns and gardens cause pollution.

Rainwater picks up chemicals as it runs over the ground. The water carries the chemicals into rivers and lakes. This is not good for fish and other animals.

rainwater

Some garden chemicals cause pollution. Others are safe for Earth.

Still, people can do many things to help Earth.

Getting energy can make air pollution. So using less energy keeps the air cleaner.

You can use less energy in your home. Turn off lights and TVs when you are not using them.

You can use less energy by cutting down on car trips. Can you walk or bike to places near your home?

There are other ways you can help keep Earth clean.

Get some friends together to clean up litter.

Look around.

How else can you help to keep Earth clean?

These kids are working together to pick up trash on a beach.

Five Ways to Help Earth

1 Don't litter.
Talk to adults about
safe ways to pick up litter.

2 Recycle and buy
recycled products.
Recycling cuts down
on trash.

5 Plant a tree. Trees help keep air clean.

4 Turn off lights, TVs, and computers that you are not using.

3 Carpool to cut down on car trips. Bike or walk when you can.

YOUR NEW WORDS

chemicals (**kem**-uh-kuhls) substances that are mixed together to make many different products

garbage (**gar**-bij) things that are thrown away

litter (**lih**-tur) papers, cans, or other garbage that is thrown on the ground

pollution (puh-**loo**-shuhn) harmful materials that damage Earth's air, water, or soil

rainwater (**rayn**-waw-tur) water that falls from the sky and collects in puddles or runs off into a body of water

soil (soyl) the dirt in which plants grow

stream (streem) a body of flowing water, like a small river

FOUR POLLUTION-FIGHTING INVENTIONS

Electric car

Solar plane

Soybean-oil-powered bus

Pedal-powered bus

23

INDEX

FIND OUT MORE

Book:

Binns, Tristan Boyer. *Clean Planet: Stopping Litter and Pollution.* Chicago: Heinemann Library, 2005.

Website:

Environmental Kids Club
http://www.epa.gov/kids

MEET THE AUTHOR

Peggy Hock lives near San Francisco, California. She likes to go backpacking in the mountains of the Sierra Nevada with her husband and two grown children. She recycles and makes sure not to litter.